100 facts

VIKINGS

100 facts

VIKINGS

Fiona Macdonald

Consultant: Jeremy Smith

Miles Kelly

First published in 2004 by Miles Kelly Publishing Ltd
Harding's Barn, Bardfield End Green, Thaxted, Essex, CM6 3PX

Copyright © Miles Kelly Publishing Ltd 2004

This edition printed in 2019

8 10 12 14 15 13 11 9

Publishing Director Belinda Gallagher
Creative Director Jo Cowan
Editorial Assistant Carly Blake
Volume Designer Louisa Leitao
Indexer Jane Parker
Reprographics Stephan Davis,

Production Elizabeth Collins, Jennifer Brunwin-Jones
Assets Lorraine King

ISBN 978-1-78617-071-2

Printed in China

British Library Cataloguing-in-Publication Data
A catalogue record for this book is available from the British Library

ACKNOWLEDGEMENTS
The publishers would like to thank the following artists
who have contributed to this book:

Peter Dennis/Mike Foster/Richard Hook/Kevin Maddison/Janos Marffy
Alessandro Menchi/Peter Sarson/Mike Saunders/Mike White/Rudi Vizi

Cartoons by Mark Davis at Mackerel

The publishers would like to thank the following sources
for the use of their photographs:

Cover: (front) Guiziou Franck/Superstock, (bg) Ella Hanochi/Shutterstock.com,
(back, t) Asmus Koefoed/Shutterstock.com

Every effort has been made to acknowledge the source and copyright holder of each picture.
Miles Kelly Publishing apologizes for any unintentional errors or omissions.

Made with paper from a sustainable forest

www.mileskelly.net

Contents

Who were the Vikings?

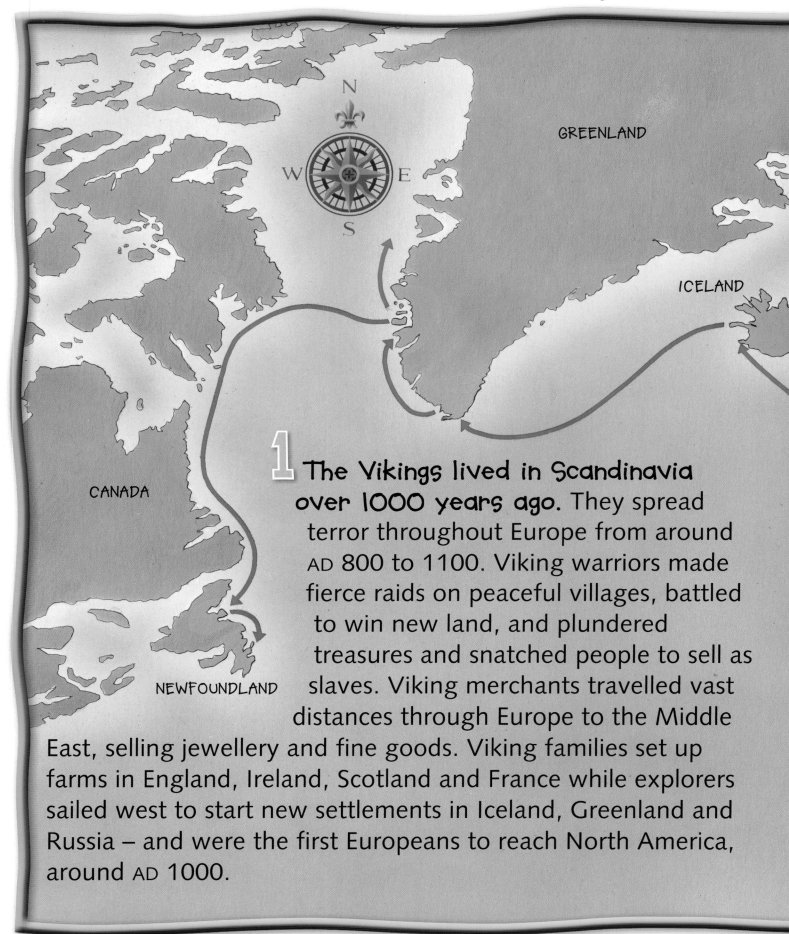

GREENLAND

ICELAND

CANADA

NEWFOUNDLAND

1 **The Vikings lived in Scandinavia over 1000 years ago.** They spread terror throughout Europe from around AD 800 to 1100. Viking warriors made fierce raids on peaceful villages, battled to win new land, and plundered treasures and snatched people to sell as slaves. Viking merchants travelled vast distances through Europe to the Middle East, selling jewellery and fine goods. Viking families set up farms in England, Ireland, Scotland and France while explorers sailed west to start new settlements in Iceland, Greenland and Russia – and were the first Europeans to reach North America, around AD 1000.

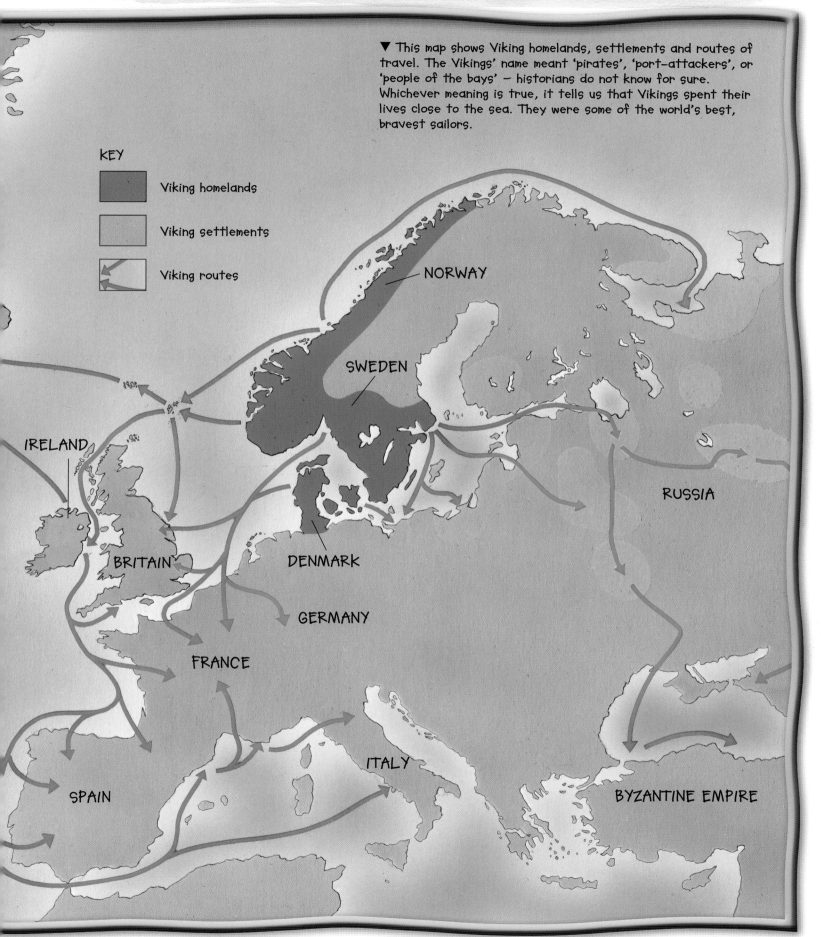

▼ This map shows Viking homelands, settlements and routes of travel. The Vikings' name meant 'pirates', 'port-attackers', or 'people of the bays' — historians do not know for sure. Whichever meaning is true, it tells us that Vikings spent their lives close to the sea. They were some of the world's best, bravest sailors.

KEY

Viking homelands

Viking settlements

Viking routes

NORWAY

SWEDEN

IRELAND

RUSSIA

BRITAIN

DENMARK

GERMANY

FRANCE

ITALY

SPAIN

BYZANTINE EMPIRE

Kings and people

2 **Viking society had three classes.** At the top were nobles (kings or chiefs). They were rich, owned land and had many servants. Freemen, the middle group, included farmers, traders, and craftworkers and their wives. Slaves were the lowest group. They worked hard for nobles and freemen and could not leave their owner.

Viking slave

Viking farmer

Viking noble warrior

▲ Slaves, farmers and warriors all worked hard to make Viking lands rich and powerful.

◄ Famous for his cruelty, Erik Bloodaxe was the last Viking to rule the kingdom of Northumbria, in north-east England.

3 **Viking warlords turned into kings.** During early Viking times, local chiefs controlled large areas of land. They also had armies of freemen. Over the centuries, some nobles became richer and more powerful than the rest by raiding and conquering foreign lands. By AD 1050, just one noble controlled each Viking country, and called himself king.

4 **King Erik Bloodaxe killed his brothers.** When a Viking king died, each of his sons had an equal right to inherit the throne. Members of Viking royal families often had to fight among themselves for the right to rule. In AD 930, King Erik of Norway killed his brothers so that he could rule alone.

5 **King Harald Bluetooth left a magnificent memorial.**
King Harald ruled Denmark from around AD 935 to 985. He was
one of the first Viking kings to become a Christian. He built
a church at Jelling, the ancient Danish royal burial
site, and had his parents' bodies dug up and
re-buried inside. He also paid for a splendid
pyramid-shaped monument to be built
next to the church, in memory of
them. This 'Jelling Stone' was
decorated with carvings in Viking
and Christian designs.

▶ The Jelling stone (far right)
has carvings of a snake and a
lion-like monster, fighting each
other. They symbolize the
forces of good and evil.

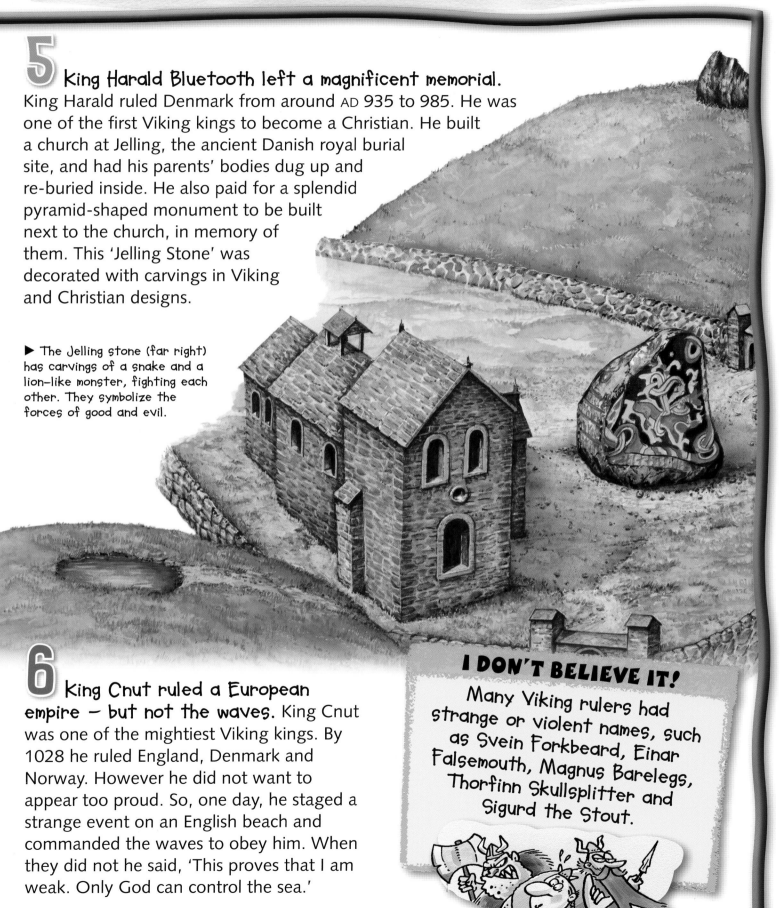

6 **King Cnut ruled a European
empire – but not the waves.** King Cnut
was one of the mightiest Viking kings. By
1028 he ruled England, Denmark and
Norway. However he did not want to
appear too proud. So, one day, he staged a
strange event on an English beach and
commanded the waves to obey him. When
they did not he said, 'This proves that I am
weak. Only God can control the sea.'

I DON'T BELIEVE IT!
Many Viking rulers had
strange or violent names, such
as Svein Forkbeard, Einar
Falsemouth, Magnus Barelegs,
Thorfinn Skullsplitter and
Sigurd the Stout.

Sailors and raiders

7 Vikings sailed in dragon ships. There were different kinds of ships. Cargo ships were slow and heavy, with wide, deep hulls to carry loads. Ferry and river boats were small and sturdy, with lots of room for passengers. The most splendid ships were *drakkar* (dragon ships), designed for war. They were long, slender and fast, with a beautifully carved stern and prow. Their shallow keels helped them land quickly on beaches to make raids.

Steering oar at stern

Rowers sat on benches, one man to each oar

QUIZ

1. What were *drakkar*?
2. When did Svein Forkbeard rule Denmark?
3. What kind of wood was used to make the keel of a boat?

Answers:
1. Viking ships 2. AD 985–1014 3. Oak

8 Sailors steered by the stars. The Vikings had no radio or satellite systems to help them navigate (steer a course) when they were out of sight of land. So they made careful observations of the Sun by day and the stars by night, to work out their position. They also studied the winds, waves and ocean currents, and the movements of fish and seabirds.

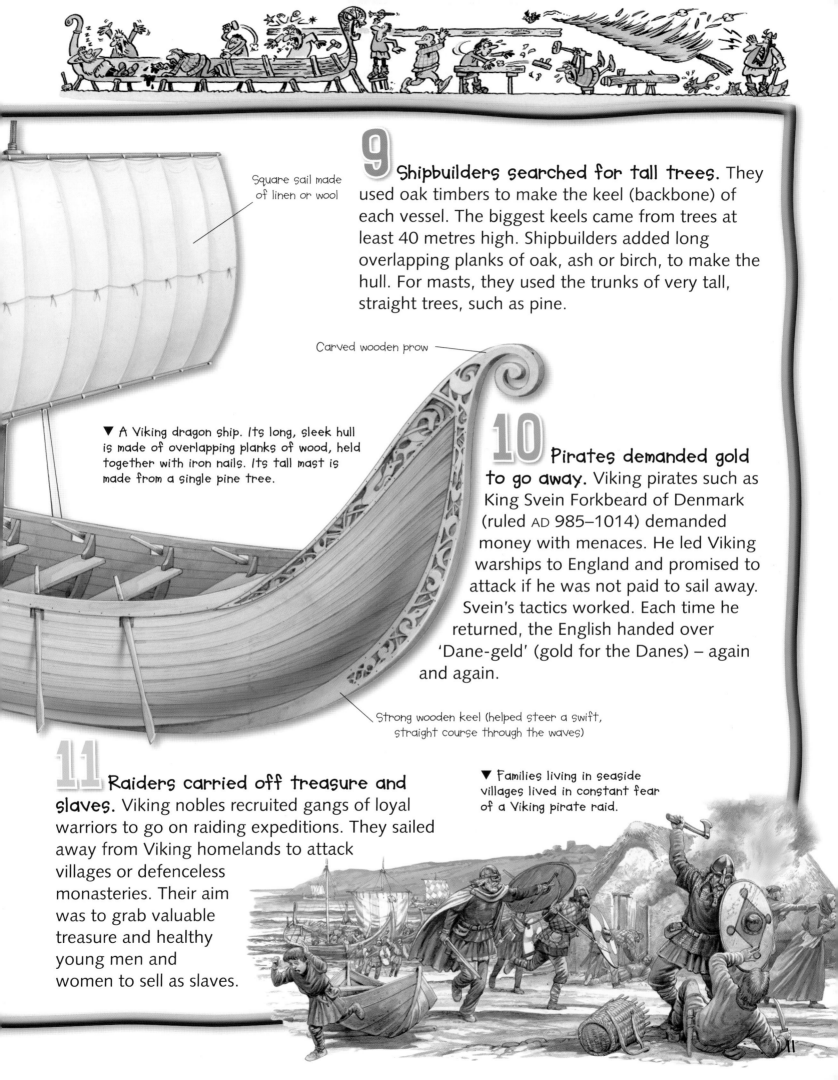

Square sail made of linen or wool

9 Shipbuilders searched for tall trees. They used oak timbers to make the keel (backbone) of each vessel. The biggest keels came from trees at least 40 metres high. Shipbuilders added long overlapping planks of oak, ash or birch, to make the hull. For masts, they used the trunks of very tall, straight trees, such as pine.

Carved wooden prow

▼ A Viking dragon ship. Its long, sleek hull is made of overlapping planks of wood, held together with iron nails. Its tall mast is made from a single pine tree.

10 Pirates demanded gold to go away. Viking pirates such as King Svein Forkbeard of Denmark (ruled AD 985–1014) demanded money with menaces. He led Viking warships to England and promised to attack if he was not paid to sail away. Svein's tactics worked. Each time he returned, the English handed over 'Dane-geld' (gold for the Danes) – again and again.

Strong wooden keel (helped steer a swift, straight course through the waves)

11 Raiders carried off treasure and slaves. Viking nobles recruited gangs of loyal warriors to go on raiding expeditions. They sailed away from Viking homelands to attack villages or defenceless monasteries. Their aim was to grab valuable treasure and healthy young men and women to sell as slaves.

▼ Families living in seaside villages lived in constant fear of a Viking pirate raid.

11

Warriors and weapons

12 Vikings valued glory more than long life.
They believed that a dead warrior's fame
lived on after him, and made sure that
his name would never die. Myths and
legends also told how warriors
who died in battle would go to
Valhalla, where they feasted
with the gods.

13 Berserkirs were mad for battle.
Berserkirs ('bear-shirts') were warriors who dressed in
animal skins and worked themselves into a trance
before battle. They charged at the enemy, howling and
growling like wolves and biting at their shields. In this
state, they were wild and fearless and dangerous to
anyone who got in their way. This is where the word
'beserk' comes from.

▲ Berserkir warriors
rushed madly into
battle, wearing animal
skins over their chain
mail armour.

14 **Lords led followers into war.** There were no national armies in Viking times. Each king or lord led his followers into battle against a shared enemy. A lord's followers fought to win praise, plus rich rewards, such as arm rings of silver or a share of captured loot.

15 **Warriors gave names to their swords.** A good sword was a Viking warrior's most treasured possession. He gave it a name such as 'Sharp Biter', and often asked to be buried with it. Viking swords were double-edged, with strong, flexible blades made by hammering layers of iron together. Their hilts (handles) were decorated with patterns in silver and gold.

16 **Viking soldiers lived in camps and forts.** Wars and raids took warriors far from home. Soldiers in places such as England built camps of wooden huts, surrounded by an earth bank topped by a wooden wall.

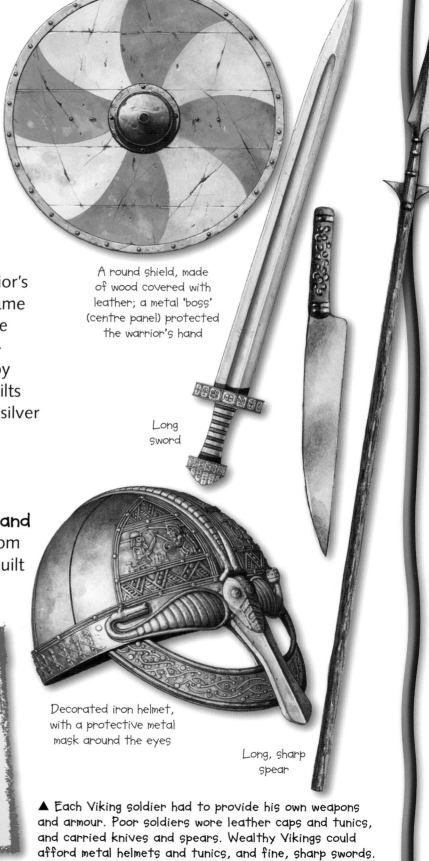

A round shield, made of wood covered with leather; a metal 'boss' (centre panel) protected the warrior's hand

Long sword

Decorated iron helmet, with a protective metal mask around the eyes

Long, sharp spear

▲ Each Viking soldier had to provide his own weapons and armour. Poor soldiers wore leather caps and tunics, and carried knives and spears. Wealthy Vikings could afford metal helmets and tunics, and fine, sharp swords.

I DON'T BELIEVE IT!

Viking women went to war but they did not fight. Instead, they nursed wounded warriors and cooked meals for hungry soldiers.

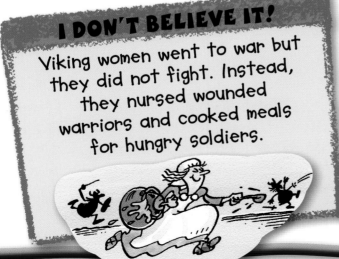

Traders, explorers, settlers

17 **Viking traders rode on camels and carried their ships.** The Vikings were brave adventurers, keen to seek out new land, slaves and treasures. Some traders travelled through Russia to Constantinople (now Istanbul in Turkey), and Jerusalem (in Israel). Each journey took several years. In Russia, they carried their ships over ground between rivers. In the desert near Jerusalem, they rode on camels, like local traders.

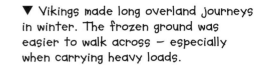

▼ Vikings made long overland journeys in winter. The frozen ground was easier to walk across — especially when carrying heavy loads.

◄ Viking merchants carried scales and weights with them on their travels.

18 **Traders carried scales and silver.** Vikings traded with many different peoples. Some used coins for trading, others preferred to barter (swap). There were no banks in Viking times and traders could not be sure of having the right money for every business deal. So they bought and sold using pieces of silver, which they weighed out on delicate, portable scales.

19 **Traders came home with lots of shopping.** Viking merchants purchased goods, as well as selling them. They went to Britain to buy wheat and woollen cloth, and to France for wine and pottery. They bought glass in Germany, jewellery in Russia, and spices from the Middle East.

QUIZ

20 **Vikings settled from Scotland in the north of Europe to Sicily in the south.** Everywhere they went, Vikings founded new villages and towns. Sometimes they fought for land from local people, but sometimes, they lived peacefully alongside them.

21 **Settlers were tricked into moving to Greenland.** Erik the Red first reached the island of Greenland around AD 983. It was bleak and icy, with little pasture, and almost no land suitable for grain. But Erik wanted families to join his new settlement. So he called it 'Greenland'. In AD 986, Viking settlers sailed to join him. By the time they discovered what Greenland was really like, it was too late to turn back.

▶ The Vikings settled on Greenland's coastline as the inland areas were covered in ice. These settlements died out between 1480 and 1500 when the climate became even colder.

22 **Vikings sailed to America — by mistake.** In AD 986, Bjarni Herjolfsson was blown off course in a storm. He saw land, but did not stop to explore. A few years later, Greenland settler Lief Eriksson decided to look for the land Bjarni had seen. He landed in places he called Hellulland, Markland and Vinland. Today, we know that these are places on the east coast of North America.

The Vikings at home

23 In the 700s and 800s, the Vikings were some of the best craftworkers in Europe. They lived in a harsh environment, with cold, long, dark winters. Buildings were needed to shelter livestock, as well as people. In towns, pigs, goats and horses were kept in sheds, but in parts of the countryside, farmers built longhouses, with rooms for the family at one end and space for animals at the other.

24 Vikings built houses out of grass. In many lands where the Vikings settled, such as the Orkney Islands or Iceland, there were hardly any trees. So Viking families built homes out of slabs of turf (earth with grass growing in it), arranged on a low foundation of stone. If they could afford it, they lined the rooms with planks of wood imported from Scandinavia. Otherwise, they collected pieces of driftwood washed up on shore.

Animals were kept in the longhouse

Loom for weaving cloth

Walls made of logs

▶ Longhouses were usually built on sloping ground so that waste from the animals ran downhill, away from human living quarters.

25 **Viking homes could be unhealthy.** Their houses did not have windows – they would have let in too much cold. So homes were often damp, and full of smoke from the fire burning on the hearth. As a result, Viking people suffered from chest diseases. Some may also have been killed by a poisonous gas called carbon monoxide, which is produced when a fire uses up all the oxygen in a room.

26 **Homeowners sat in the high seat.** Most Viking families had little furniture. Only the rich could afford beds, or tables with fixed legs. Most homes were simply furnished with trestle tables, wooden storage chests and wooden benches. The centre of one bench was marked off by two carved wooden pillars, and reserved as the 'high seat' (place of honour) for the house owner. Important guests sat facing him or her, on the bench opposite.

Turf (earth with growing grass) roof

Wooden rafters

Meat was smoked to preserve it

Outside lavatory

Farmers, fishers and hunters

27 **Viking farmers prized pasture more than ploughed fields.** In northern lands, the soil was too thin and stony for crops such as wheat and barley to grow well. Farmers relied on sheep and cattle to provide meat and milk. These animals needed fresh grass to eat so Viking farmers valued pasture land, where grass flourished, more than stony fields.

28 **Flax and hay were the most important crops.** They were needed to make clothes and feed cattle. Outer garments were made of wool, and could be very itchy, so women wove smoother, finer cloth to wear next to the skin. They used the stalks of a plant called flax, which farmers planted in damp ground. Farm animals needed hay (dried grass) to eat in winter, when pastures were covered by snow. Viking farmers grew grass in well-manured meadows, then cut it, dried it and stored it for winter.

Fish drying in the wind

Rack for drying grass to make hay

29 **Hunters and fishermen found food around the coast.** The Vikings lived close to some of the world's richest fishing grounds. Fishermen used nets and traps to catch sea fish such as cod and herring, or river fish such as salmon, trout and eels. They gathered mussels and oysters from the seashore, and hunted whales, mostly for their blubber (fat). Young men climbed dangerous cliffs to collect seabirds and their eggs or scrambled over skerries – little rocky islands – to catch seals and walruses basking there.

◀ The Vikings were not just interested in raiding and stealing. They realized that the British Isles provided good farmland and safe areas for settlements.

Ships anchored in a safe harbour

Cutting grass to make hay

Ploughing with oxen

Scattering grain to feed chickens

30 **Trappers tracked wild animals.** In Norway and Sweden, there were many wild animals, such as bears, wolves and foxes. These were hunted for their furs, which made warm clothes, or were sold to rich customers. Deer were also hunted for their meat, antlers and skins. Antlers were used to make beads and combs.

Food and famine

31 **Vikings ate two meals a day.** First thing in the morning was the 'day meal' of barley bread or oatcakes, and butter or cheese. The main meal – 'night meal' – was eaten in the early evening. It included meat or fish, plus wild berries in summer. Meals were served on wooden plates or soapstone bowls and eaten with metal knives and wood or horn spoons.

Patterned silver cup used by the rich

▶ Objects made from cattle horn were light but very strong – ideal for Viking traders or raiders to carry on their journeys.

Pottery beaker used by the poor

Drinking horn used by warriors

QUIZ

1. What did Viking warriors drink from?
2. How did the Vikings boil water?
3. What is offal?
4. How long would a feast last for?

Answers:
1. From cattle horns
2. On red-hot stones 3. The heart, liver and lungs of animals 4. A week or more

32 **Warriors drunk from hollow horns.** Favourite Viking drinks were milk, whey (the liquid left over from cheese-making), ale (brewed from malted barley), and mead (honey wine). Rich people drank from glass or silver cups, but ordinary people had wooden or pottery beakers. On special occasions feasts were held, and Viking warriors drank from curved cattle horns.

33 Red-hot stones boiled water for cooking. Few Viking homes had ovens. So women and their servants boiled meat in iron cauldrons, or in water-filled pits heated by stones that were made red-hot in a fire. This was a very efficient way of cooking.

▲ Vegetables eaten by Vikings included peas, beans, cabbages, onions and garlic.

34 The Vikings loved blood sausages. Cooks made sausages by pouring fresh animal blood and offal (heart, liver and lungs) into cleaned sheep's intestines, then boiling them. Sometimes they added garlic, cumin seeds or juniper berries as flavouring. Vikings preferred these to vegetables such as cabbages, peas and beans.

▼ Viking women and slaves cooked huge meals over open fires, and served them to feasting warriors.

35 Feasts went on for a week or more. After winning a great victory, Vikings liked to celebrate. Kings and lords held feasts to reward their warriors, and families feasted at weddings. Guests dressed in their best clothes and hosts provided plenty of food and drink. Everyone stayed in the feast hall until the food ran out, or they grew tired.

Women and children

36 Viking women were independent. They made important household decisions, cooked, made clothes, raised children, organized slaves and managed farms and workshops while their husbands were away.

▲ Women spun sheep's wool and wove it into warm cloth on tall, upright looms.

MAKE A VIKING PENDANT

You will need:

string or cord 40 centimetres long   modelling clay   white, yellow and brown paint   gold and silver paint   paintbrush

1. Shape some animal fangs from modelling clay, about 4 centimetres long.
2. Make a hole through the widest end of each fang. Leave to harden.
3. Paint the fangs with white, brown or yellow paint. When dry, decorate with gold and silver paint.
4. Thread string through the fangs and wear around your neck like a Viking.

37 Only widows could wed who they wanted to. If a Viking man wanted to marry, he had to ask the young woman's father for permission and pay him a bride price. If the father accepted this, the marriage went ahead, even if the woman did not agree. Widows had more freedom. They did not need anyone's permission to marry again. Viking laws also gave all women the right to ask for a divorce if their husbands treated them badly.

38 Old women won respect for wise advice.

Many Viking women died young in childbirth or from infectious diseases. So older people, aged 50 or more, were a small minority in Viking society. While they were still fit, they were respected for their knowledge and experience. But if they grew sick or frail, their families saw them as a burden.

39 Viking fathers chose which children survived.

Parents relied on children to care for them in old age so they wanted strong offspring. The father examined each baby after it was born. If it seemed healthy, he sprinkled it with water and named it to show it was part of his family. If the child looked sickly he told slaves to leave it outside to die.

◀ Feeding chickens and collecting eggs was work for Viking girls. They learned how to grow vegetables and cook by helping their mothers.

40 Viking children did not go to school.

Daughters helped their mothers with cooking and cleaning, fed farm animals, fetched water, gathered wood, nuts and berries and learned how to spin, weave and sew. Sons helped their fathers in the workshop or on the farm. They also learned how to ride horses and use weapons. Boys had to be ready to fight by the time they were fifteen or sixteen years old.

▲ Viking boys practised fighting with wooden swords and small, lightweight shields.

Clothes and jewellery

41 **Vikings wore lots of layers to keep out the cold.** Women wore long dresses of linen or wool with woollen over-dresses. Men wore wool tunics over linen undershirts and woollen trousers. Both men and women wore gloves, cloaks, socks, and leather boots or shoes. Men added fur or sheepskin caps while women wore headscarves and shawls.

▶ Viking men and women liked bright colours and patterns. They often decorated their clothes with strips of woven braid.

42 **Furs, fleeces and feathers also helped Vikings keep warm.** Vikings lined or trimmed their woollen cloaks with fur, or padded them, like quilts, with layers of goose-down. Some farmers used sheepskins to make cloaks that were hard-wearing, as well as very warm.

43 **Brooches held Viking clothes in place.** There were several different styles. Men wore big round brooches, pinned on their right shoulders, to hold their cloaks in place. Women wore pairs of brooches – one on each shoulder – to fasten the straps of their over-dresses. They might also wear another brooch at their throat, to fasten their cloak, plus a brooch with little hooks or chains, to carry their household keys.

▶ This beautiful brooch, decorated with real gold wire, was once worn by a very rich Viking nobleman.

44 **Rings showed Vikings' wealth – and bravery.** Viking men, as well as women, liked to wear lots of jewellery. They thought it made them look good, but it also displayed their wealth, and sometimes, their achievements. Arm- and neck-rings, in particular, were often given to warriors as rewards for fighting bravely in battle.

▼ Viking craftworkers used designs from many different lands to create beautiful jewellery.

Arm-ring of twisted gold

Russian-style necklace of silver and rock crystal

Gold brooch with long pin – a typical British style

Small gold ring

45 **Favourite Viking clothing colours were red and green.** Archaeologists have found the remains of brightly-coloured cloth at Viking sites. They have also found fragments of patterned braid, silk ribbon, and gold and silver thread. All were used to decorate Viking clothes.

I DON'T BELIEVE IT!

The Vikings imported boatloads of broken glass from Germany, to melt and make into beautiful glass beads.

Health and beauty

46 **The English complained that Vikings were too clean.** They said that the Vikings combed their hair, changed their clothes and bathed too often. Vikings bathed by pouring water over red-hot stones to create clouds of steam. They sat in the steam to sweat, then whipped their skin with birch twigs to help loosen the dirt. Then they jumped into a pool of cold water to rinse off.

▲ Vikings 'bathed' in clouds of steam. Similar steam baths, called saunas, are still popular in Scandinavia today.

47 **Some Vikings took their swords to the lavatory.** Most Viking homes had an outside lavatory, consisting of a bucket or a hole in the ground with a wooden seat on top. The lavatory walls were often made of wickerwork – panels of woven twigs. But Viking warriors in enemy lands made different arrangements. They went outside in groups of four, carrying swords to protect one another.

▲ Viking lavatories may have looked like this. Vikings used dried moss, grass or leaves as toilet paper.

48

Vikings used onions to diagnose illness. If a warrior was injured in the stomach during a battle, his comrades cooked a dish of porridge strongly flavoured with onion and gave it to him to eat. They waited, then sniffed the wound. If they could smell onions, they left the man to die. They knew that the injury had cut open the stomach, and the man would die of infection.

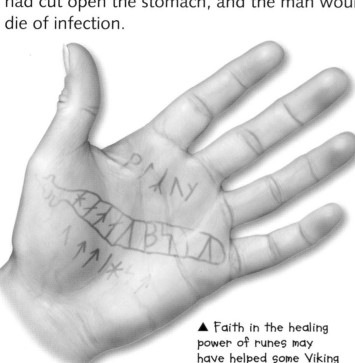

▲ Faith in the healing power of runes may have helped some Viking people feel better.

49

For painkilling power, the Vikings relied on runes. The Vikings made medicines from herbs and other plants, but they also believed that runes – their way of writing – had magic healing powers. They carved runic spells and charms on pieces of bone and left them under the heads of sleeping sick people. Runes were written on women's palms during childbirth to protect from pain.

50

Hair-care was very important. Viking women wore their hair long. They left it flowing loose until they married, then tied it in an elaborate knot at the nape of their neck. Viking men also liked fancy hairstyles. They cut their hair short at the back, but let their fringes grow very long. So that they could see where they were going, some Vikings plaited the strands that hung down either side of their face.

▲ Fashionable Viking hairstyles. Women also wove garlands of flowers to wear in their hair on special occasions.

Skilled craftworkers

51 **Vikings made most of the things they needed.** Families had to make – and mend – almost everything, from their houses and furniture to farm carts, clothes and children's toys. They had no machines to help them, so most of this work was done slowly and carefully by hand.

▼ Blacksmiths heated iron over open fires until it was soft enough to hammer into shape to make tools and weapons.

52 **Blacksmiths travelled from farm to farm.** Many Viking men had a simple smithy at home, where they could make and mend tools. For specialized work, they relied on skilled blacksmiths who travelled the countryside, or they made a long journey to a workshop in a town.

53 Bones could be beautiful.

Skilled craftworkers used deer antlers to make fine combs. But these were too expensive for ordinary Vikings to buy. They carved bones left over from mealtimes into combs, beads and pins, as well as name tags and weaving tablets (used to make patterned braid).

54 Craftsmen carved cups from the cliff face.

Deposits of soft soapstone were found in many Viking lands. It looked good, but it was very heavy. To save taking lumps of it to their workshops, stoneworkers carved rough shapes of cups and bowls into cliffs at soapstone quarries, then took them home to finish neatly.

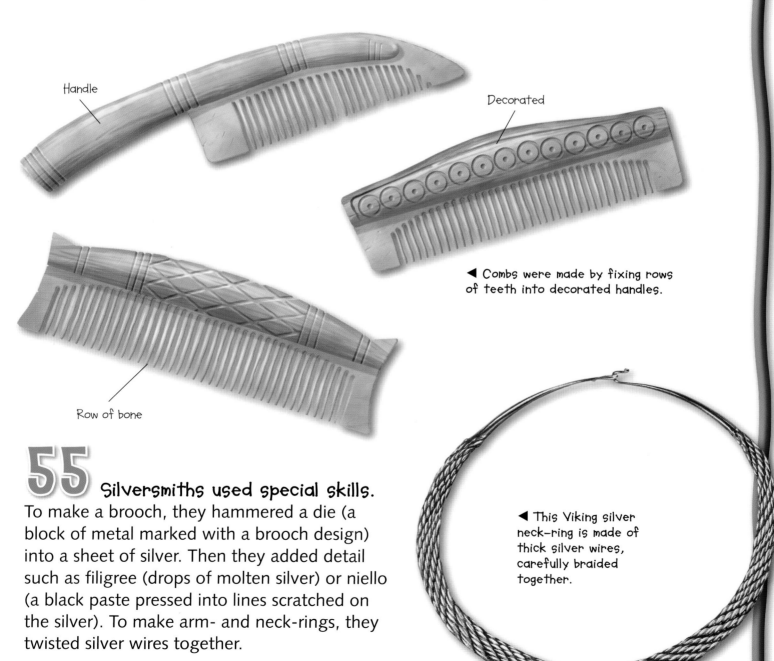

Handle

Decorated

Row of bone

◄ Combs were made by fixing rows of teeth into decorated handles.

55 Silversmiths used special skills.

To make a brooch, they hammered a die (a block of metal marked with a brooch design) into a sheet of silver. Then they added detail such as filigree (drops of molten silver) or niello (a black paste pressed into lines scratched on the silver). To make arm- and neck-rings, they twisted silver wires together.

◄ This Viking silver neck-ring is made of thick silver wires, carefully braided together.

Viking towns

56 Kings built towns to encourage trade. Before the Vikings grew so powerful, merchants traded at fairs held just once or twice a year. Viking kings decided to build towns so that trade could continue all year round. Taxes were collected from the people and merchants who traded there.

▶ Viking markets were often held on beaches. Farming families and travelling merchants met there to buy and sell.

57 Towns were tempting targets for attack. Pirates and raiders from Russia and north Germany sailed across the Baltic Sea to snatch valuable goods from Viking towns. So kings paid for towns to be defended with high banks of earth and strong wooden walls. They also sent troops of warriors to guard them.

58 Houses in towns were specially designed. Space was limited inside town walls so houses were built close together. They were smaller than country homes, as people needed less space to store crops or house animals. Most town houses were made of wood with thatched roofs. Many had craft workshops and showrooms inside.

I DON'T BELIEVE IT!

The first Russians were Vikings. The name 'Russia' comes from the word, 'Rus', used by people living east of the Baltic Sea to describe Viking traders who settled there.

59 Towns made the first Viking coins.

As far as we know, there were no coins in Scandinavia before the Viking age. Traders bartered (swapped) goods, or paid for them using bits of silver, weighed out on tiny, portable scales. But many foreign coins came to Viking lands from overseas trading and raiding. Around AD 825, craftsmen in the Viking town of Hedeby (now in north Germany) began to copy them. Later, other towns set up mints to make coins of their own.

60 Viking traders gave Russia its name.

Adventurous Vikings visiting the east shores of the Baltic set up towns as bases for trade. Some of the biggest were Staraja Ladoga and Novgorod, in Russia, and Kiev in Ukraine.

◀ This Viking coin shows a merchant ship. It comes from the town of Hedeby.

Law and order

61 Vikings followed a strict code of honour. Men and women were proud and dignified and honour was important to them. It was a disgrace to be called a cheat or a coward, or to run away from a fight. Vikings also prized loyalty. They swore solemn promises to be faithful to lords and comrades and sealed bargains by shaking hands.

62 Many quarrels were settled by fighting. Quarrels between Viking families often led to feuds. If one family member was insulted or killed, all others had a duty to avenge him. Feuds could continue for months, with many people on both sides being killed, until each family was prepared to seek peace and pay compensation.

▲ Viking warriors challenged people who insulted them – or harmed their families – to a deadly duel.

63 **Viking laws were not written down.** Instead, they were memorized by a man known as the law-speaker. He recited them out loud every year so that everyone else could hear and understand them. Because of their expert knowledge, law-speakers often became advisors to kings and lords.

64 **Every year, Vikings met at the Thing.** This was an open-air assembly of all free men in a district. It met to punish criminals and make new laws. The most usual punishments were heavy fines. Thing meetings were great social occasions where people from remote communities had the chance to meet and exchange news. Many traders also attended, setting up stalls with goods around the edge of a field.

▼ All free men – from noble chieftains to farmers – could speak and vote at a Viking Thing.

65 **Ruthlessness was respected.** It was tough being a Viking. Everyone had to work hard to survive and there was no room in the community for people who were weak, lazy or troublesome. Thieves were often hanged and criminals who refused to pay compensation or fines were outlawed. This was a very harsh penalty. Without a home and family, it was hard for any individual to survive.

QUIZ

1. What were the two worst Viking punishments for crimes?
2. How did the Vikings settle family feuds?
3. Why did Vikings shake hands with each other?
4. Who recited the Viking laws?

Answers:
1. Hanging and being outlawed
2. By fighting 3. To seal bargains
4. The law-speaker

Games, music and sport

▲ Vikings loved magical, mysterious tales of dragons, elves and monsters — and exciting stories about famous local heroes.

66 **Vikings liked music, dancing and clowns.** At feasts, Vikings sang songs and danced. Depending on how much the guests had drunk, the dancing might be slow or riotous. Kings and lords also paid dancers, clowns, acrobats and jugglers to entertain their guests at feasts.

67 **Vikings laughed at jokes and riddles.** The Vikings had a rough, quick-witted sense of humour. They liked playing practical jokes and listening to stories about gods and heroes who defeated enemies by trickery. Vikings also played dice and board games such as chess and 'hneftafl' (king's table). But they were not good losers. Fighting often broke out at the end of a game.

▶ This board and counters were probably used for playing the game 'hneftafl', which was rather like chess.

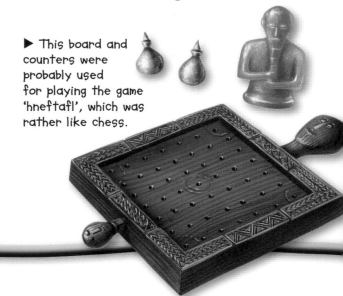

68 Swimming, racing and jumping were favourite summer games. In summer, the weather was warm enough for Vikings to take off most of their clothes. This made it much easier for people to move freely and run and jump at greater speed. In winter, warmly-dressed Vikings liked snow-based sports such as cross-country skiing, as well as ice skating on frozen rivers and lakes.

▼ Viking archers used bows made of yew wood, strung with twisted plant fibres. Arrows were made of birch wood, with sharp tips made of iron.

69 Viking sports were good training for war. Spear-throwing, sword-fighting and archery (shooting at targets with bows and arrows) were all popular Viking sports. They were also excellent training in battle skills and helped boys and young men to develop their body strength, get used to handling weapons and improve their aim.

70 Vikings liked watching wrestling — and fights between horses. Wrestling matches were also good training for war. A warrior who lost his weapons might have to fight for his life on the battlefield. But many Vikings watched wrestling just for fun. They enjoyed the violence. They also liked to watch brutal fights between stallions (male horses), who attacked one another with hooves and teeth.

Gods and goddesses

71 **Viking people honoured many gods.** The Aesir (sky gods) included Odin, Thor and Tyr, who were gods of war, and Loki, who was a trickster. The Vanir (gods of earth and water) included Njord (god of the sea) and Frey (the farmers' god). He and his sister Freyja brought pleasure and fertility.

▼ Odin, Viking god of war, rode an eight-legged horse. Two ravens, called Thought and Memory, flew by his side.

▼ Beautiful Viking goddess Freyja rode in a chariot pulled by cats.

72 **Animals – and people – were killed as sacrifices.** The Vikings believed that they could win favours from the gods by offering them gifts. Since life was the most valuable gift, they gave the gods living sacrifices. Vikings also cooked meals of meat – called blood-offerings – to share with the gods.

73 **Destiny controlled the Vikings.** According to legends, three sisters (Norns) decided what would happen in the world. They sat at the foot of Yggdrasil, the great tree that supported the universe, spinning 'the thread of destiny'. They also visited each newborn baby to decide its future. Once made, this decision could not be changed.

74 **After death, Vikings went to Hel's kingdom.** Vikings believed that warriors who died in battle went to Valhalla or to Freyja's peaceful home. Unmarried girls also joined Freyja, and good men went to live with gods in the sky. Most Vikings who lived ordinary lives and died of illness or old age could only look forward to a future in Niflheim. This was a gloomy place, shrouded in fog, ruled by a fierce goddess called Hel.

▶ Vikings asked fierce and furious god Tyr to help them win victories.

75 **Towards the end of the Viking age, many people became Christians.** Missionaries from England, Germany and France visited Viking lands from around AD 725. The Vikings continued to worship their own gods for the next 300 years. Around AD 1000, Viking kings such as Harald Bluetooth and Olaf Tryggvason decided to follow the Christian faith to help strengthen their power. They built churches and encouraged people to become Christians.

▼ Njord was god of the sea. He married the giantess Skadi, who watched over snowy mountains.

QUIZ

1. Who was Loki?
2. What was the name of the tree that was said to support the universe?
3. Where did warriors go when they died?

Answers:
1. A trickster god
2. Yggdrasil 3. Valhalla

Heroes, legends and sagas

76 **Vikings honoured heroes who died in battle.** They told stories, called 'sagas', about their adventures so that their name and fame never died. These stories were passed on by word of mouth for many years. After the end of the Viking Age, they were written down.

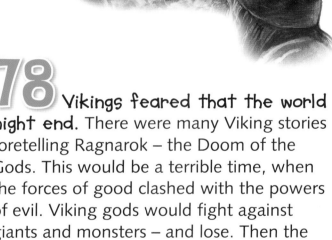

▶ Vikings loved sagas – stories that recorded past events and famous peoples' lives.

77 **Skalds sang songs and told saga stories.** Viking kings and lords employed their own personal poets, called skalds. A skald's job was to sing songs and recite poems praising his employer, and to entertain guests at feasts. Most skalds played music on harps or lyres to accompany their poems and songs.

▼ Viking legends told how the world would come to an end at the battle of Ragnarok. They also promised that a new world would be born from the ruins of the

78 **Vikings feared that the world might end.** There were many Viking stories foretelling Ragnarok – the Doom of the Gods. This would be a terrible time, when the forces of good clashed with the powers of evil. Viking gods would fight against giants and monsters – and lose. Then the world would come to an end.

79

The Vikings believed in spirits and monsters. They were unseen powers that lived in the natural world. Some, such as elves, were kindly and helpful. They sent good harvests and beautiful children. Others, such as giants who ate humans, were wicked or cruel. Vikings often imagined monsters as looking like huge, fierce animals. They carved these monster heads on ships and stones to scare evil spirits away.

▲ Vikings believed that Valkyries — wild warrior women — carried men who had died in battle to live with Odin in Valhalla (the hall of brave dead).

◄ A Viking silver amulet (lucky charm), shaped like Thor's hammer.

QUIZ

1. What did Vikings call the end of the world?
2. Who did skalds praise?
3. Why did farmers wear hammers round their necks?
4. Where did Vikings carve the heads of monsters?

Answers:
1. Ragnarok 2. Their employer 3. To bring fertility to their fields and animals 4. On ships and stones

80

Lucky charms protected warriors and farmers. They wore amulets shaped like the god Thor's magic hammer as pendants around their necks. Warriors believed that these amulets would give them strength in battle. Farmers hoped they would bring fertility to their fields and animals.

Death and burial

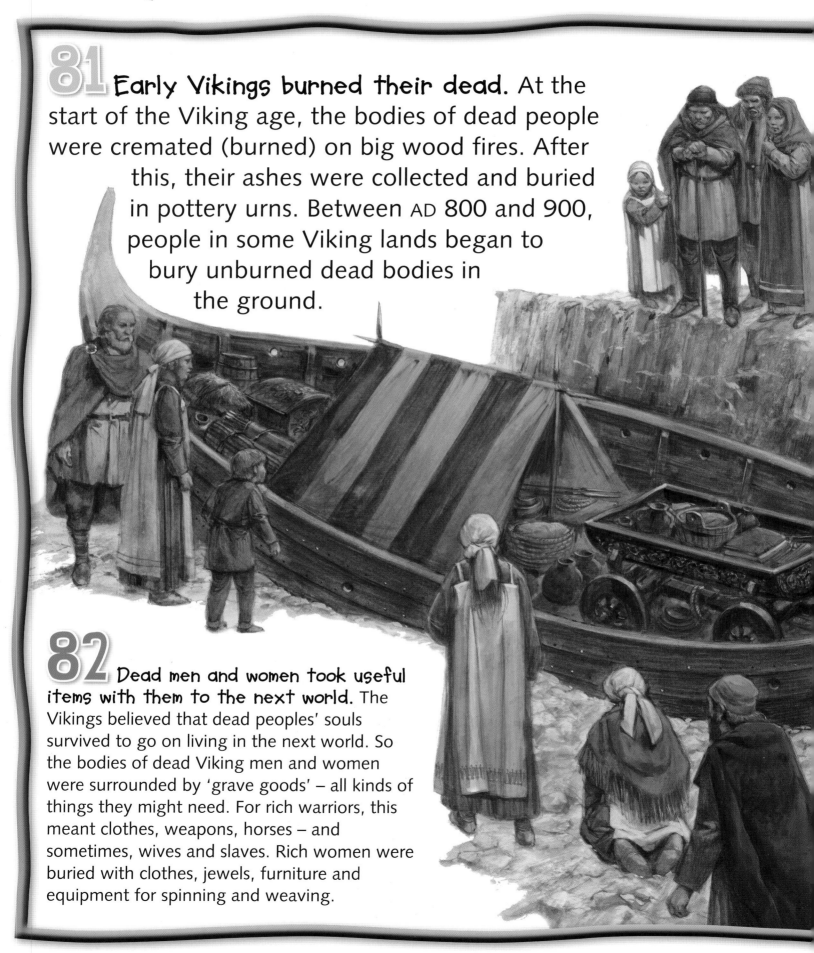

81 **Early Vikings burned their dead.** At the start of the Viking age, the bodies of dead people were cremated (burned) on big wood fires. After this, their ashes were collected and buried in pottery urns. Between AD 800 and 900, people in some Viking lands began to bury unburned dead bodies in the ground.

82 **Dead men and women took useful items with them to the next world.** The Vikings believed that dead peoples' souls survived to go on living in the next world. So the bodies of dead Viking men and women were surrounded by 'grave goods' – all kinds of things they might need. For rich warriors, this meant clothes, weapons, horses – and sometimes, wives and slaves. Rich women were buried with clothes, jewels, furniture and equipment for spinning and weaving.

83
Viking graves have survived for hundreds of years. Archaeologists have discovered many collections of grave contents, in remarkably good condition. Some, such as jewellery, pottery and stone carvings, are made of materials that do not rot. Some, such as clothing, have survived by chance. Others, such as ship burials, have been preserved underwater. All have provided valuable evidence about life in Viking times.

▼ These stones arranged in the shape of a ship's hull mark an ancient Viking burial ground.

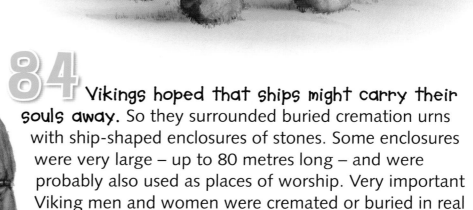

84
Vikings hoped that ships might carry their souls away. So they surrounded buried cremation urns with ship-shaped enclosures of stones. Some enclosures were very large – up to 80 metres long – and were probably also used as places of worship. Very important Viking men and women were cremated or buried in real wooden ships, along with valuable grave goods.

◀ The dead were laid to rest in cloth-covered shelters on board real ships. Then the ships were set on fire so that their souls could 'sail away' to the next world.

85
Vikings treated dead bodies with great respect. They washed them, dressed them and wrapped them in cloth or birch bark before burying them or cremating them. This was because the Vikings believed that dead people might come back to haunt them if they were not treated carefully.

I DON'T BELIEVE IT!
Some Viking skeletons and wooden ships that were buried in acidic soils have been completely eaten away. But they have left 'shadows' in the ground, which archaeologists can use to find out more about them.

Writing and picture stories

86 **Many ordinary Vikings could not read or write.** They relied on the spoken word to communicate and on memory to preserve details of land, family histories and important events. At the beginning of the Viking age, all Vikings spoke the same language, the 'donsk tunga' (Danish Tongue). But after around AD 1000, different dialects developed.

▲ Viking runes. From top left, these symbols stand for the sounds: F U Th A R K H N I A S T B M L R.

87 **Viking scribes wrote in runes.** There were 16 letters, called runes, in the Viking alphabet. They were used for labelling valuable items with the owner's name, for recording accounts, keeping calendars and for sending messages. Runes were written in straight lines only. This made them easier to carve on wood and stone. The Vikings did not have paper.

▼ Vikings used sharp metal points to carve runes on useful or valuable items.

Deer antler with runes carved on it

Viking calendar

Comb with runes showing owner's name

88 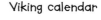 **Runes were used to cast magic spells.** Sometimes, runes were used to write messages in secret code, or even magic spells. These supposedly gave the objects they were carved on special power. Some secret Viking writings in runes still have not been deciphered today.

89

Rune stones told stories. Wealthy families paid for expert rune masters to carve inscriptions on stones, praising and commemorating dead parents and children. Some boastful people also had stones carved with details of their own achievements. When the carvings were completed, the rune stones were raised up in public places where everyone could see them.

◀ Rune stones were written records of Viking citizens.

90

Picture stones told of great adventures. In some Viking lands, people carved memorial stones with pictures, instead of runes. These showed scenes from the dead person's life and details of their adventures, together with pictures of gods, giants and monsters.

WRITE YOUR NAME IN RUNES

Use the chart on page 42 to try to write your name in runes.

The Viking alphabet was called 'futhark', after its first six letters. It had a special letter for the sound 'th' and no letters for the sounds 'e' and 'o'. Even the Vikings found it difficult to write some names and words!

◀ Some picture stones told of people's achievements, others commemorated loved ones who had died.

The end of the Vikings

91 **Kings defeated Viking power.** For centuries, kings in England, Scotland and Ireland failed to drive the Vikings from their lands. But after AD 1000, they began to succeed. Brian Boru, high king of Ireland, defeated the Vikings in 1014, and Viking rule ended in England in 1042. Kings of Norway, descended from Vikings, ruled parts of Scotland until 1266 and the Orkney and Shetland Islands until 1469.

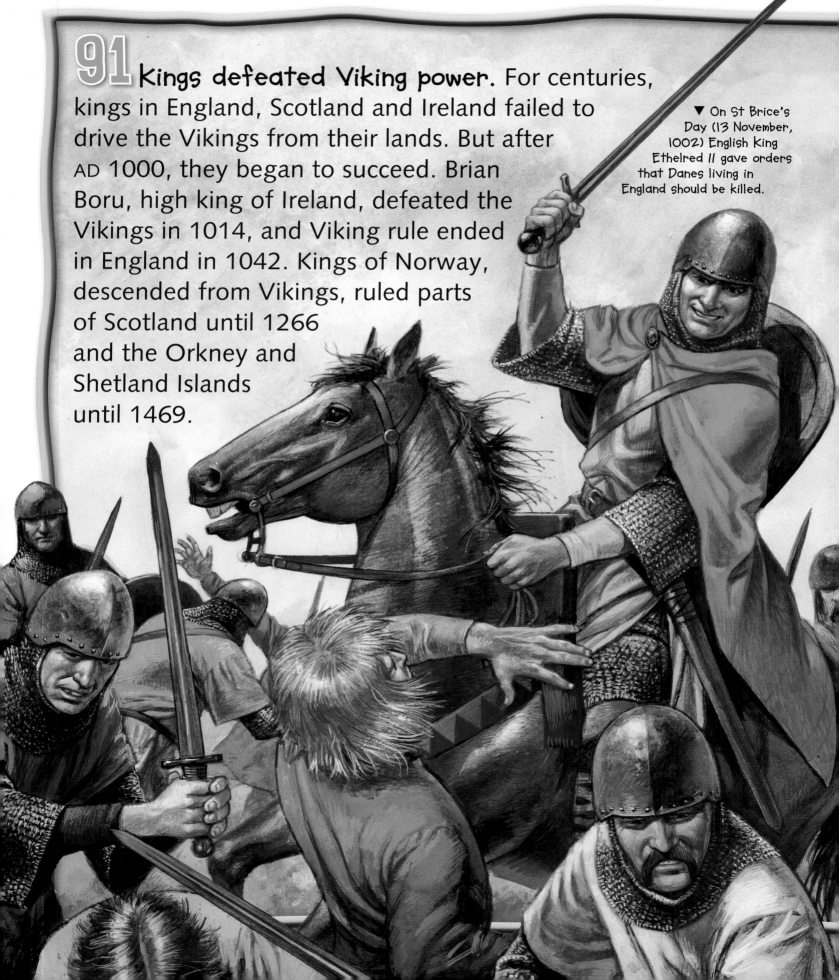

▼ On St Brice's Day (13 November, 1002) English King Ethelred II gave orders that Danes living in England should be killed.

92 **Vikings learned to live alongside other peoples.** In most places where Vikings settled, they married local women and worked with local people. Some of their words and customs blended with local ones, but many disappeared. Viking traditions only survived if the place where they settled was uninhabited, such as Iceland, or the Orkney Islands, off the north of Scotland.

▲ In 1066, the Normans – descendants of Vikings who had settled in Normandy, France – invaded and conquered England. This scene from the huge Bayeux Tapestry (embroidered wall–hanging) shows their Viking–style ships.

93 **Christianity destroyed faith in Viking gods.** The Vikings believed their gods, such as Thor and Odin, would punish them if they did not worship them, and would kill Christian missionaries. But the missionaries survived, and so did Vikings who became Christians. This made other Vikings wonder if their gods had any powers, at all.

◄ Christians living in Scandinavia after the end of the Viking age made statues of Jesus Christ to stand in their churches, as symbols of their faith.

94 **Vikings set up new kingdoms outside Viking lands.** In places far away from the Viking homelands, such as Novgorod in Russia, or Normandy in northern France, Viking warlords set up kingdoms that developed independently. Over the years, they lost touch with their Viking origins, and created new customs, laws and lifestyles of their own.

95 **Viking settlers abandoned America.** Soon after AD 1000, Thorfinn Karlsefni, a Viking merchant from Iceland, led over 100 Viking men and women to settle at Vinland – the site in North America where Lief Eriksson landed. They stayed there for two years, but left because the native people attacked them and drove them away.

Viking survivals

96 **Some days of the week still have Viking names.** The Vikings honoured different gods on different days of the week. We still use some of these gods' names in our calendars. For example, Wednesday means 'Woden's Day', Thursday means 'Thor's Day' and Friday means 'Freyja's Day'. In modern Scandinavian languages, Saturday is called 'bath-day', because that was when the Vikings had their weekly bath!

97 **We still use many Viking words today.** In countries where the Vikings settled, they spoke Viking languages and gave Viking names to their surroundings. Many Viking words for everyday things still survive such as 'sister', 'knife' and 'egg'. Many places in northern Europe still have Viking names, such as 'Thorpe' (outlying farm), Firth (river estuary), Cape Wrath (Cape Turning-point) or 'Kirkwall' (Church-bay).

98 **A Viking story inspired Shakespeare's most famous play.** William Shakespeare (1564–1616) lived over 500 years after the Vikings. He used one of their stories to provide the plot for one of his best-known plays. It tells the story of Hamlet, a prince in Denmark, who cannot make up his mind what to do after his father is murdered.

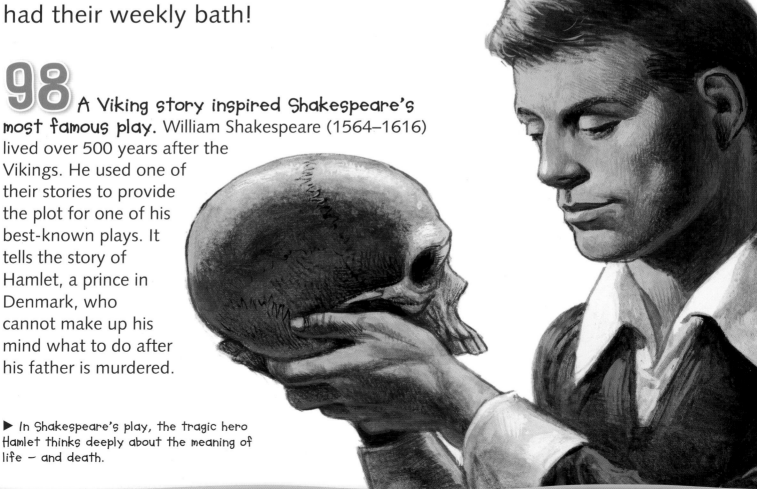

▶ In Shakespeare's play, the tragic hero Hamlet thinks deeply about the meaning of life – and death.

99 People still celebrate Viking festivals. For example, in the Shetland Isles, where many Vikings settled, people celebrate 'Up-Helly-Aa' on the last Tuesday in January. This marks the end of Yule, the Viking mid-winter festival. They dress up as Vikings, parade through the streets, then burn a lifesize model of a Viking warship.

100 Father Christmas was originally a Viking god. Yule (mid-winter) was one of the most important Viking festivals. It was a time when Vikings held feasts and exchanged presents. They also believed that Viking gods travelled across the sky, bringing good things – just like Father Christmas!

▶ Today, as in Viking times, the light and warmth of blazing fires at mid-winter festivals bring hope and cheerfulness at a cold, dark time.

▲ This modern picture of Father Christmas shows him riding through the sky in a Viking-style sleigh, pulled by reindeer from Viking lands.

Index

Entries in **bold** refer to main subject entries. Entries in *italics* refer to illustrations.